Financial Education Top

Practical Guide to Achieving Excellent Financial Education

A. Luvaren

Copyright © 2024

Practical Guide

1. Introduction

Financial education is an increasingly relevant topic in a world where the conscious management of personal and collective economic resources is crucial for individual and social well-being. This text will explore in detail the definition and importance of financial education, its history, and the main objectives it aims to achieve.

Definition and Importance of Financial Education

Definition:

Financial education can be defined as the process through which individuals and communities acquire the knowledge, skills, and attitudes necessary to make informed and conscious decisions regarding money management. This process includes learning the basics of economics, such as saving, investing, debt management, and retirement planning, as well as understanding more complex concepts such as financial markets, inflation, portfolio diversification, and risk management.

Financial education is not limited to merely acquiring technical knowledge; it also involves developing a mindset oriented toward prudence, responsibility, and foresight. In other words, financial education encompasses the skills that allow individuals to manage their financial resources effectively to achieve short-, medium-, and long-term goals, avoid financial pitfalls, and build a secure and stable economic future.

Importance:

The importance of financial education is hard to overestimate. In an increasingly complex and globalized economic context, where financial products are becoming more diversified and accessible, a lack of financial skills can have serious consequences. These include over-indebtedness, poor future planning, inefficiency in saving, and the inability to take advantage of investment opportunities.

1. **Prevention of Over-Indebtedness:** Adequate financial education enables individuals to understand the importance of living within their means and avoiding over-indebtedness. This is particularly crucial in an era where credit is easily accessible, often with negative consequences for those unable to manage it correctly.

2. **Promotion of Saving and Investment:** Financial education teaches the importance of saving and sound money management practices, such as setting aside funds for emergencies or saving for future goals. It also helps individuals understand the basics of investing, allowing them to grow their wealth in a safe and informed manner.

3. **Awareness and Protection from Financial Risks:** Understanding the risks associated with different financial products and investments is a crucial part of financial

education. This includes the ability to assess risks and benefits, as well as recognizing financial scams and protecting oneself from them.

4. **Planning for the Future:** Financial education includes planning for the future, such as preparing for retirement or children's education. With good financial planning, individuals can ensure a stable economic life even in times of uncertainty.

5. **Social and Economic Integration:** Financial education is a key factor in economic and social integration. People who understand fundamental financial concepts are better equipped to make decisions that improve their quality of life and contribute to the overall well-being of society.

Ultimately, financial education is a vital skill that should be taught from a young age, as it influences every aspect of life, from managing daily expenses to planning for the future and participating actively in the global economy.

History of Financial Education

Although financial education may seem like a modern concept, it has deep historical roots. Examining its evolution can help us better understand how it has become a fundamental discipline in today's society.

1. Ancient Origins:

The foundations of financial education can be traced back to ancient civilizations. For example, the Babylonians, known for their Code of Hammurabi, had developed a complex system of economic laws regulating loans, debts, and interest rates. This code reflected an awareness of the importance of rules and guidelines for managing economic resources. Even in ancient Greece and the Roman Empire, there were financial systems that required a certain understanding of economic operations, such as trade and credit.

2. Middle Ages and Renaissance:

During the Middle Ages, financial education was primarily linked to the aristocracy and merchants. Italian city-states like Venice and Florence were centers of trade and finance, and saw the development of the first banks. Successful merchants needed a deep knowledge of economic operations, accounting, and risk, skills that were often passed down through apprenticeships.

With the Renaissance, there was a revival of interest in economics and finance, spurred by the expansion of trade and the early forms of capitalism. Aristocratic and bourgeois families began educating their children in finance, as money management became an increasingly important aspect of daily life and business activities.

3. The Industrial Revolution:

The Industrial Revolution marked a significant change in the economic structure of society. With urbanization and the expansion of factories, many people suddenly found themselves involved in a market economy that required a new understanding of financial matters. It was during this period that the first forms of organized financial education began to spread.

The growing availability of credit and the need to save for the future led to the creation of the first savings banks and credit unions, which often also played an educational role, teaching their members the basics of money management.

4. 20th Century:

The 20th century saw an explosion in access to financial products and a growing recognition of the importance of financial education. During the Great Depression of the 1930s, millions of people lost their savings due to bank collapses, an event that highlighted the need for a greater understanding of the financial system.

In the post-World War II period, with the expansion of the consumer economy and the introduction of credit cards, financial education became even more relevant. In the 1970s and 1980s, with the liberalization of financial markets, the complexity of financial products increased, making it essential for consumers to understand how these instruments worked.

It was in this context that a global movement began to promote financial education at all levels of society. International organizations such as the OECD (Organization for Economic Co-operation and Development) started working with governments to develop educational programs aimed at improving financial awareness.

5. 21st Century:

In the 21st century, financial education has become a priority for many countries and international organizations. The global financial crisis of 2008 highlighted the serious consequences of a lack of financial education, with millions of people worldwide losing homes, savings, and jobs due to poorly informed financial decisions.

In response to this crisis, many governments launched initiatives to improve the financial education of their citizens. In the United States, for example, the government created the Financial Literacy and Education Commission, which works to promote financial awareness. Similarly, in Europe, the European Commission has supported various projects aimed at improving financial education across all member countries.

Today, financial education is recognized as a fundamental element for social inclusion and economic well-being. Schools in many countries have begun to include financial education courses in their programs, recognizing that a solid foundation of financial skills is essential for preparing students for a responsible and autonomous adult life.

Objectives of Financial Education

The objectives of financial education can be divided into several categories, each aimed at developing specific skills and promoting healthy financial behaviors. These objectives range from simple money management to long-term financial planning and active participation in the economic system.

1. Improving Money Management:

One of the main objectives of financial education is to provide individuals with the skills necessary to effectively manage their money. This includes teaching fundamental concepts such as creating a budget, managing expenses, and the importance of saving.

- **Creating and Managing a Budget:** Teaching individuals how to create and maintain a budget is fundamental to effective financial management. A well-structured budget helps monitor income and expenses, allowing people to live within their means and save for future goals.

- **Systematic Saving:** Another objective is to encourage regular saving, both for emergencies and long-term projects. Financial education teaches the importance of setting aside a portion of income to build a financial safety net.

- **Debt Reduction and Management:** In an era where credit is easily accessible, it is crucial to educate people about the dangers of debt and how to manage it responsibly. This includes teaching techniques for reducing debt, such as paying off credit cards in full each month, and understanding the implications of interest rates.

2. Promoting Long-Term Financial Planning:

Another key objective of financial education is to help people plan for their financial future. This includes planning for retirement, children's education, home purchase, and other major financial decisions.

- **Retirement Planning:** It is essential for individuals to understand the importance of saving for retirement and the different options available, such as private pension plans and company pension funds. Good retirement planning ensures a comfortable life after retirement, avoiding financial difficulties.

- **Investments:** Financial education aims to provide the necessary skills to understand and manage investments. This includes understanding different types of investments (stocks, bonds, mutual funds, real estate), the associated risks and benefits, and the importance of diversification to minimize risks.

- **Purchasing High-Value Assets:** Financial education helps prepare for major purchases, such as buying a home or car. This involves understanding the financing process, negotiating loan terms, and evaluating the sustainability of such purchases relative to one's budget.

3. Increasing Awareness of Financial Risks:

Another objective is to increase awareness of financial risks and provide the skills to manage them.

- **Risk Management:** Financial education teaches individuals to recognize the risks associated with different financial decisions and to take measures to mitigate them. For example, understanding the necessary insurance coverages (such as health, life, or home insurance) is essential for protecting one's assets.

- **Protection from Financial Fraud:** With the rise of scams and financial fraud, it is essential that individuals are educated on how to protect themselves from these threats. This includes understanding safe practices for using credit cards, managing passwords, and recognizing warning signs of potential scams.

4. Promoting Financial Inclusion and Economic Autonomy:

Financial education also aims to promote financial inclusion, ensuring that all individuals, regardless of their socioeconomic background, have access to the tools and knowledge needed to fully participate in the economy.

- **Access to Financial Services:** An important objective is to ensure that everyone has access to basic financial services

, such as bank accounts, credit, and insurance. Financial education helps people understand how to use these services responsibly.

- **Economic Autonomy:** Finally, financial education seeks to empower individuals to make independent and informed economic decisions, allowing them to achieve a higher level of economic autonomy. This includes the ability to negotiate financial terms, understand legal contracts, and make informed decisions about their financial future.

Conclusion

In summary, financial education is a critical discipline that has evolved over centuries, becoming increasingly relevant in today's complex and interconnected world. Its main objectives are to provide individuals with the skills and knowledge necessary to manage their money effectively, plan for the future, manage financial risks, and achieve greater economic autonomy. By achieving these objectives, financial education contributes to both individual well-being and the broader social and economic stability of communities and nations.

Next in Practical Guide

Section 2: Strategies for improving your financial habits.

2. Basic Principles of Personal Finance

Personal finance is a fundamental skill for the effective management of individual economic resources. Understanding and applying the basic principles of personal finance allows one to make informed decisions regarding their money, facilitating the achievement of both short- and long-term financial goals. This text will explore in detail the key concepts of income and expenses, saving and investing, budgeting, and the concept of interest.

Income and Expenses

Definition of Income:

Income represents the money an individual earns or receives over a certain period. This can come from various sources, including salaries, wages, bonuses, investment income, pensions, and other forms of compensation. Income is the foundation that determines the ability to save, invest, and cover daily expenses.

- **Salaries and Wages:** The most common source of income for most

people is the salary or wage earned through employment. This form of income is often regular and predictable, making financial planning easier.
- **Investment Income:** Investments can generate income in the form of dividends, interest, or capital gains. This income may be irregular and depends on the performance of the investments.
- **Pension or Annuity Income:** Individuals who are retired or who have purchased annuities may receive a regular stream of income from these sources. This income is generally predictable and can be planned to cover living expenses.
- **Other Sources of Income:** Income can also come from side activities, such as rental income from real estate, royalties from creative works, or profits from a business venture.

Definition of Expenses:
Expenses represent the money an individual spends or invests over a certain period. Expenses can be classified into two main categories: fixed expenses and variable

expenses.

- **Fixed Expenses:** Fixed expenses are those that remain constant month to month, such as mortgage or rent payments, utility bills, insurance premiums, and loan payments. These expenses are generally predictable and must be covered regularly.
- **Variable Expenses:** Variable expenses, on the other hand, can vary from month to month. Examples include grocery costs, entertainment expenses, travel, and unexpected medical costs. Managing variable expenses requires more attention, as they can significantly impact the ability to save and invest.
- **Discretionary Expenses:** Within variable expenses, there are also discretionary expenses, which are non-essential, such as dining out, luxury purchases, and entertainment. These expenses can be reduced or eliminated to increase savings or cover unexpected costs.

Managing Income and Expenses:
Effectively managing income and expenses is crucial for maintaining a healthy financial

balance. A balanced budget means that income is sufficient to cover all expenses, with a margin for savings and investments.

- **Tracking Income and Expenses:** The first step in managing personal finances is to accurately track all income and expenses. This can be done using a manual ledger, a spreadsheet, or financial management apps. Monitoring income and expenses provides a clear view of how money is being spent and helps identify areas where savings can be made.
- **Expense Management:** Reducing unnecessary expenses is one of the most effective strategies for improving one's financial situation. This could include cutting entertainment costs, reducing food expenses, or negotiating better rates for utilities and services.
- **Active Budget:** An active budget occurs when income exceeds expenses, allowing for savings and investment of the excess money. Maintaining an active budget is essential for building a solid emergency fund and planning for the future.

Saving and Investing

Saving:

Saving is the act of setting aside a portion of one's income for future use. Saving is essential for covering unexpected expenses, reaching short-term financial goals, and preparing for the future.

- **Importance of Saving:** Saving provides financial security and flexibility. Having an adequate emergency fund allows you to handle unexpected events such as job loss, emergency repairs, or medical expenses without resorting to loans or debt. A good emergency fund should cover at least 3-6 months of essential living expenses.
- **Types of Savings Accounts:** Savings accounts offer a safe place to store money. These accounts may include traditional savings accounts, high-yield savings accounts, certificates of deposit (CDs), and money market accounts. Each has different characteristics in terms of accessibility and interest rates.
- **Systematic Saving:** Saving systematically, such as setting aside a

fixed percentage of income each month, is an effective strategy for building a significant savings balance over time. Automating transfers to a savings account is a way to ensure that saving becomes a priority.

Investing:

Investing is the process of allocating resources (money) into assets that are expected to generate a return over time. Investments can vary in terms of risk and return, and include a wide range of options such as stocks, bonds, mutual funds, real estate, and other financial instruments.

- **Investment Goals:** Investments can be used for various financial goals, such as wealth accumulation, retirement, purchasing a home, or funding a child's education. Investment goals influence choices regarding the duration and level of risk of the investments.
- **Diversification:** A key principle of investing is diversification, which involves spreading investments across different asset classes (stocks, bonds, real estate, etc.) to reduce overall risk. Diversifying the portfolio helps protect

investors from significant losses in case of poor performance of a single investment.
- **Risk and Return:** Risk and return are interconnected concepts in investing. Generally, investments with a higher potential return carry a greater risk. It is important to understand your risk profile and choose investments that align with your risk tolerance and financial goals.
- **Investment Strategies:** There are various investment strategies, ranging from passive approaches (such as investing in index funds) to active approaches (such as selecting individual stocks). Other strategies include long-term investing, dollar-cost averaging (regularly investing a fixed amount), and portfolio management based on age and life stage.
- **Time and Compound Interest in Investments:** The factor of time is crucial in investments. Investing long-term allows you to benefit from compound interest, where returns generated by investments are

reinvested, generating additional returns. The longer the investment period, the greater the potential for capital growth.

Budgeting: Creation and Management

Definition of Budgeting:
Budgeting is the process of planning and controlling income and expenses. Creating and managing a personal budget is one of the most effective tools for maintaining control over your finances and achieving your financial goals.

Creating a Budget:
Creating a budget involves several key steps, including identifying income, categorizing expenses, setting savings goals, and planning for future expenses.

1. **Identifying Income:** The first step in creating a budget is to identify all sources of income. This includes net income, i.e., income that remains after deducting taxes and other mandatory withholdings.
2. **Categorizing Expenses:** Next, it is necessary to categorize all expenses into

fixed expenses (such as rent, mortgage, bills) and variable expenses (such as food, entertainment, clothing). This breakdown helps to better understand where the money goes and to identify potential areas for savings.

3. **Setting Savings Goals:** A good budget includes a section dedicated to savings. This could include savings for short-term goals (like a vacation or major purchase) and long-term savings (like a retirement fund or down payment for a house).

4. **Planning for Future Expenses:** Budgeting should also consider predictable future expenses, such as tax payments, home maintenance, or school expenses. Including these expenses in the budget helps avoid surprises and prepares you financially.

Managing the Budget:
Managing the budget means monitoring income and expenses against the spending plan and making adjustments when necessary.

- **Regular Monitoring:** It is important to monitor the budget regularly, ideally every month, to check if the plan is

being followed. This helps identify any deviations and correct errors quickly.
- **Adjustments:** If it is found that expenses exceed income or that savings are not reaching the expected level, it may be necessary to review the budget and make adjustments. This could mean reducing expenses in certain categories or finding ways to increase income.
- **Flexibility:** An effective budget is flexible and can be adapted to changing circumstances. For example, if you receive a raise, you might decide to increase savings or allocate more money to discretionary spending.

Budgeting Tools:

Today, there are numerous digital tools that make creating and managing a budget easier. These tools may include budgeting apps, spreadsheets, and financial software that help track expenses, monitor account balances, and manage savings.

The Concept of Interest

Definition of Interest:

Interest is the cost of borrowed money or the return earned on invested money. There are two main types of interest: simple interest and compound interest.

Simple Interest:

Simple interest is calculated only on the original amount invested or borrowed. For example, if you invest €1,000 at a 5% interest rate for one year, you will earn €50 in interest (€1,000 x 0.05).

- **Formula:** Simple interest is calculated with the formula:
  Simple Interest=Principal×Interest Rate ×Time\text{Simple Interest} = \text{Principal} \times \text{Interest Rate} \times \text{Time}Simple Interest=Principal×Interest Rate×Time This type of interest is commonly used for short-term loans and basic savings accounts.

Compound Interest:

Compound interest, on the other hand, is calculated on both the original principal and the accumulated interest over time. This means that interest is earned on previously earned interest, creating an exponential growth effect.

- **Formula:** Compound interest is

calculated with the formula:

$$\text{Compound Interest} = \text{Principal} \times \left(1 + \frac{\text{Interest Rate}}{\text{Number of Compounding Periods}}\right)^{\text{Number of Compounding Periods} \times \text{Time}} - \text{Principal}$$

- **Effect of Compounding:** The effect of compounding is particularly powerful in the long term. For example, investing €1,000 at a 5% interest rate compounded annually for 10 years would result in a final balance of €1,628.89 (€1,000 x (1 + 0.05)^10), demonstrating the impact of earning interest on interest.
- **Application of Compound Interest:** Compound interest is commonly used for long-term investments, such as

retirement savings accounts, investment funds, and mortgage calculations. The longer the investment period, the more significant the impact of compound interest.

Interest in Debt:

Interest also plays a crucial role in the context of debt. When borrowing money, interest represents the cost of borrowing. Understanding how interest works in loans, credit cards, and other forms of debt is essential for managing and minimizing the cost of borrowing.

- **Loan Interest:** For loans, such as mortgages or personal loans, the interest rate determines how much the borrower will pay in addition to the principal over the life of the loan. It's important to compare interest rates and loan terms to find the most affordable options.
- **Credit Card Interest:** Credit card debt typically carries high-interest rates, especially if balances are not paid in full each month. Carrying a balance on a credit card can lead to significant interest charges over time, making it a costly form of debt.

- **Impact of Interest on Debt Repayment:** Higher interest rates increase the total cost of borrowing and can prolong the time required to pay off debt. Understanding the impact of interest on debt repayment is crucial for effective debt management and for making informed decisions about borrowing.

Conclusion

Understanding the basic principles of personal finance, including the management of income and expenses, saving and investing, budgeting, and the concept of interest, is crucial for achieving financial stability and long-term financial goals. By mastering these concepts, individuals can make informed decisions that contribute to their financial well-being and future security.

3. Types of Savings and Investments

Effective personal finance management involves understanding and consciously using different types of savings and investments. Each of these options has unique characteristics in terms of accessibility, potential returns, liquidity, and risk. In this overview, we will explore in detail the main types of savings and investments, starting from traditional savings like checking accounts and deposits, moving to more complex financial instruments such as stocks, bonds, and funds, and finally reaching alternative investments like real estate and cryptocurrencies. We will also examine the fundamental relationship between risk and return, a crucial element for managing a financial portfolio.

Traditional Savings: Checking Accounts and Deposits

Checking Accounts:

Checking accounts are the most common and traditional method of saving. These are bank accounts primarily used to manage daily transactions, such as depositing salaries, paying bills, and withdrawing cash.

- **Characteristics of Checking Accounts:** Checking accounts offer high liquidity, allowing users to easily access their money through ATMs, checks, transfers, and debit cards. However, they provide very low, if not zero, returns in the form of interest. They are secure tools but are not ideal for growing capital over time.

- **Use of Checking Accounts:** While checking accounts are not investment tools, they are essential for managing daily finances. It is important to maintain a sufficient balance to cover current expenses while avoiding leaving too much inactive money, which could be better invested in higher-yielding instruments.

Savings Deposits and Savings Accounts:

Savings deposits, including savings accounts, are another type of traditional saving, primarily used to set aside money in excess of daily needs.

- **Characteristics of Savings Accounts:** Savings accounts offer a slightly higher interest rate compared to checking accounts while maintaining good liquidity. However, the returns are still generally low, and funds are almost immediately accessible. These accounts are insured by most national banking authorities, thus offering protection against capital loss.

- **High-Yield Savings Accounts:** Some savings accounts offer higher interest rates, especially those offered by online banks with lower operating costs. These accounts are ideal for savers seeking a combination of safety and higher returns compared to traditional savings accounts.

Certificates of Deposit (CDs):

Certificates of Deposit (CDs) are savings

products offered by banks that provide a higher interest rate in exchange for locking up the money for a predetermined period.

- **Characteristics of CDs:** CDs have varying terms ranging from a few months to several years. In exchange for limited access to the capital, the bank offers a fixed interest rate, generally higher than that of savings accounts. However, withdrawing money from a CD before maturity can result in significant penalties.

- **Use of CDs:** CDs are ideal for those who can afford to lock away a portion of their savings for a defined period in exchange for higher returns and capital security. They are particularly useful in a low-interest-rate environment, as they offer guaranteed returns.

Financial Instruments: Stocks, Bonds, and Funds

Stocks:

Stocks represent a share of ownership in a company and grant the holder the right to participate in the company's profits through dividends and capital appreciation.

- **Characteristics of Stocks:** Investing in stocks can offer potentially high returns but also involves significant risk, as stock values can fluctuate widely based on the company's performance and market conditions. Stocks offer two main types of returns: dividends (periodic payments made by the company to shareholders) and capital appreciation (increase in stock value over time).

- **Types of Stocks:** There are various categories of stocks, including common stocks, which provide voting rights at shareholder meetings, and preferred stocks, which do not offer voting rights but guarantee a fixed dividend. Blue-chip stocks represent solid and established companies with a long history of stability and returns, while growth stocks represent younger and expanding companies with greater growth potential but also higher risk.

- **Stock Investment Strategies:** Investors can adopt various strategies, such as long-term investing in blue-chip stocks for stability and dividends or investing in growth stocks for potential capital appreciation. Diversifying the portfolio is crucial to mitigating the risks associated with stock investments.

Bonds:

Bonds are debt securities issued by governments, public entities, or companies, representing a loan made by the investor to the issuer in exchange for regular interest payments and the return of the principal at maturity.

- **Characteristics of Bonds:** Bonds are considered fixed-income instruments as they offer regular interest payments (coupons) and the return of the principal at a specified date. However, the market value of bonds can vary depending on interest rates and the issuer's creditworthiness.

- **Types of Bonds:** There are various types of bonds, including government bonds (such as U.S. Treasury Bonds), corporate bonds, and municipal bonds. Government bonds are generally considered safer, while corporate bonds offer higher yields but with a greater risk of default.

- **Bond Risk and Return:** Bond yields are influenced by market interest rates and the issuer's credit rating. Lower-rated bonds (junk bonds) offer higher returns in exchange for greater default risk. Investors must carefully evaluate the risk before investing in high-yield bonds.

Mutual Funds:

Mutual funds pool money from many investors to purchase a diversified portfolio of stocks, bonds, or other financial instruments, managed by a team of professionals.

- **Characteristics of Mutual Funds:** Mutual funds offer diversification, as the money invested is spread across a large number of securities, reducing the specific risk of each security. Investors purchase shares of the fund, whose value is tied to the overall performance of the portfolio.

- **Types of Mutual Funds:** There are various types of mutual funds, including equity funds, bond funds, balanced funds (which combine stocks and bonds), and sector funds (which invest in specific sectors of the economy). Index funds, which replicate the performance of a market index like the S&P 500, are popular for their simplicity and low management costs.

- **Advantages and Disadvantages of Mutual Funds:** Mutual funds offer easy access to financial markets and are suitable for less experienced investors. However, management fees and commissions can erode returns. Investors should choose funds with a good track record and low management costs.

Exchange-Traded Funds (ETFs):

ETFs are similar to mutual funds but are traded like stocks on a stock exchange. ETFs offer diversification and flexibility, combining the benefits of mutual funds and stocks.

- **Characteristics of ETFs:** ETFs replicate the performance of an index, a sector, or a specific set of assets and can be bought and sold in real-time during market hours. They are generally characterized by lower fees compared to mutual funds.

- **Advantages of ETFs:** ETFs offer transparency, as investors can see real-time market prices and the value of the underlying portfolio. They also provide greater flexibility in buying and selling compared to mutual funds, making them ideal for active investors.

**Alternative Investments: Real Estate

and Cryptocurrencies**

Real Estate Investments:

Real estate investment involves purchasing, managing, and selling real estate properties to generate income and/or capital appreciation.

- **Types of Real Estate Investments:** Real estate investments can include the purchase of residential, commercial properties, or land. Investors can earn through property rentals or selling at a higher price than the purchase price.

- **Characteristics of Real Estate Investments:** Real estate is considered a tangible and relatively safe investment, with the potential to generate steady passive income. However, it requires significant initial capital, maintenance and management costs, and is less liquid compared to other investments.

- **Real Estate Investment Trusts (REITs):** REITs are companies that own, manage, or finance income-producing real estate. Investing in REITs allows investors to participate in the real estate market without directly purchasing property. REITs offer liquidity, as they are traded on the stock exchange, and diversification, but like any investment, they also carry risks related to real estate market fluctuations.

Cryptocurrencies:

Cryptocurrencies are digital assets that use cryptography to secure transactions and control the creation of new units. Bitcoin is the first and most well-known cryptocurrency, but there are thousands, each with unique characteristics.

- **Characteristics of Cryptocurrencies:** Cryptocurrencies are decentralized and not controlled by governments or central banks. They are highly volatile, with wide price fluctuations, and are used both as a medium of exchange and as a store of value.

- **Investing in Cryptocurrencies:** Investing in cryptocurrencies is seen by many as an opportunity to achieve high returns in a short time, but it also involves high risk. The volatility of the cryptocurrency market makes this type of investment suitable only for investors willing to tolerate significant losses.

- **Non-Fungible Tokens (NFTs) and Decentralized Finance (DeFi):** Other emerging aspects of cryptocurrencies include NFTs, which represent unique digital ownership of artwork or other digital assets, and DeFi, which refers to blockchain-based financial platforms offering services such as loans and exchanges without traditional intermediaries.

Risk and Return: Understanding the Relationship

Definition of Risk and Return:

Risk is the probability that an investment may lose value, while return is the reward an investor receives for taking that risk. There is a direct relationship between risk and return: investments with higher risk generally offer higher potential returns, while safer investments tend to offer lower returns.

- **Market Risk:** Market risk concerns fluctuations in the value of an investment due to changes in economic, political, or social conditions. This type of risk cannot be eliminated through diversification.

- **Specific Risk:** Specific risk is related to a single investment or company, such as a company's bankruptcy or a sector crisis. This risk can be mitigated through portfolio diversification.

Balancing Risk and Return:

Investors must balance risk and return based on their financial goals, time horizon, and risk tolerance. For example, a young investor with a long time horizon might choose riskier investments but with higher potential returns, while an investor nearing retirement might prefer safer investments.

- **Diversification:** Diversification is a strategy to reduce risk by spreading investments across different asset classes and sectors. A diversified portfolio might include a combination of stocks, bonds, real estate, and alternative investments.

- **Investor Risk

 Profiles:** Investors can be classified into different profiles based on their risk tolerance, ranging from conservative (low-risk, low-return) to aggressive (high-risk, high-return). Understanding one's own risk profile is crucial to selecting appropriate investments.

Choosing between different types of savings and investments is a critical aspect of personal finance management. From traditional tools such as checking accounts and savings deposits to more complex instruments like stocks, bonds, mutual funds, ETFs, and alternative investments like real estate and cryptocurrencies, each option has unique characteristics in terms of risk, return, and liquidity. A solid understanding of these options and the relationship between risk and return will enable investors to make informed decisions and build a balanced financial portfolio that meets their goals and needs.

4. Financial Planning in Adulthood

Financial planning in adulthood is a fundamental process for ensuring long-term economic stability and well-being. This stage of life is characterized by crucial financial decisions that require careful consideration and strategic resource management. In this overview, we will examine the key aspects of financial planning for adults, including setting financial goals, creating an emergency savings plan, and planning for retirement. Understanding and applying these concepts can help build a solid foundation for financial security in the future.

Setting Financial Goals

Importance of Goal Setting:

Setting clear financial goals is the first step in financial planning. Goals provide clear direction and motivation for saving and investing, allowing you to make informed decisions about how to manage your money.

- **Short-, Medium-, and Long-Term Goals:** Financial goals can be categorized based on their time horizon. Short-term goals, such as buying a car or saving for a vacation, usually take a few months to a couple of years. Medium-term goals, like purchasing a home or funding a child's education, can take 3 to 10 years. Long-term goals, such as retirement planning, extend beyond 10 years.

- **SMART Goals:** An effective method for defining financial goals is the SMART model, which suggests creating goals that are Specific, Measurable, Achievable, Realistic, and Time-bound. For example, instead of setting a generic goal like "saving for retirement," a SMART goal could be "saving €200,000 for retirement within 20 years by contributing €500 per month to a pension fund."

Assessing the Current Financial Situation:

Before setting goals, it is essential to assess the current financial situation, including income, expenses, debts, savings, and investments. This assessment helps understand the capacity for saving and investing and identifies any problem areas.

- **Cash Flow Analysis:** A detailed cash flow analysis allows you to see how money is managed each month, highlighting income and expenditures. This step is crucial for identifying waste and savings opportunities.

- **Personal Balance Sheet:** The personal balance sheet summarizes what you own (assets) and what you owe (liabilities). Subtracting liabilities from assets gives the net worth, an indicator of overall financial health.

Prioritizing Goals:

After defining goals, it is important to prioritize them based on their urgency and importance. Not all goals can be achieved simultaneously, so strategic choices are necessary.

- **Balancing Goals:** For example, it may be necessary to balance saving for an emergency fund with saving for retirement. Short-term goals might require immediate attention, but it is also essential not to neglect long-term goals.

- **Flexibility and Goal Review:** Financial goals should be flexible and adaptable to life changes, such as a new job, marriage, or the birth of a child. It is important to periodically review goals and the financial plan to ensure they remain aligned with current circumstances.

Emergency Savings Plan

Importance of an Emergency Fund:

An emergency fund is a crucial element of financial planning, as it provides a safety net in case of unexpected events, such as job loss, sudden medical expenses, or urgent home repairs.

- **Purpose of the Emergency Fund:** The emergency fund is designed to cover essential expenses in case of income disruption. This helps avoid relying on high-interest debt, such as credit cards, which can jeopardize long-term financial stability.

- **Size of the Emergency Fund:** The general rule is to set aside an amount equivalent to 3-6 months of essential expenses. However, the ideal size of the emergency fund may vary based on personal factors, such as job stability, the number of dependents, and the level of risk tolerance.

Strategies for Building an Emergency Fund:

Building an emergency fund requires discipline and planning. While it may seem challenging to set aside a significant amount, this goal can be achieved through a series of gradual steps.

- **Set a Savings Goal:** Start by setting a specific goal for the emergency fund, for example, €10,000. This goal can be broken down into smaller, manageable milestones, such as saving €1,000 per month for 10 months.

- **Create an Automatic Savings Plan:** Set up a monthly automatic transfer from your checking account to a dedicated emergency savings account. This removes the temptation to spend the money intended for the emergency fund.

- **Cut Non-Essential Expenses:** Identify non-essential expenses that can be reduced or temporarily eliminated to contribute to the emergency fund. For example, it might be helpful to forgo dining out or unnecessary subscriptions until the savings goal is reached.

Managing the Emergency Fund:

Once built, the emergency fund must be carefully managed to ensure it remains available when needed.

- **Where to Keep the Emergency Fund:** The emergency fund should be kept in an accessible and secure savings account, preferably with a competitive interest rate. Avoid investing the emergency fund in volatile financial instruments, as the priority is liquidity and security, not returns.

- **Using the Emergency Fund:** The emergency fund should only be used for genuinely unforeseen situations, not for planned expenses or desires. It is important to replenish the fund as soon as possible after using it.

Retirement Planning

Importance of Retirement Planning:

Retirement planning is one of the most important aspects of financial planning. With increasing life expectancy and uncertainty about public pensions, it is essential to build a solid retirement plan to ensure a comfortable standard of living in the post-working years.

- **Starting Early:** The earlier you start planning for retirement, the greater the impact of compounding interest on savings. Even small regular contributions can grow significantly over time thanks to compound interest.

- **Determining Retirement Needs:** To plan effectively, you need to estimate financial needs during retirement. This includes evaluating current expenses, predicting any lifestyle changes, and considering inflation and healthcare.

Tools for Retirement Planning:

Employer-Sponsored Pension Plans:

Many companies offer pension plans as part of the compensation package. These plans can vary significantly, but the most common include defined contribution plans, such as 401(k) plans in the United States, and defined benefit plans, such as corporate pensions.

- **Defined Contribution:** In defined contribution plans, employees contribute a portion of their salary to a retirement account, often with a matching contribution from the employer. The money is invested in a portfolio of assets, and the final balance depends on the investment performance. It is important to contribute at least the percentage needed to obtain the maximum employer contribution, as this is a significant benefit.

- **Defined Benefit:** Defined benefit plans, less common today, offer a fixed income during retirement, usually calculated based on years of service and the average salary of the last years of work. These plans provide greater certainty than defined contribution plans but also require prudent management by companies.

Individual Retirement Accounts:

In addition to employer plans, it is possible to contribute to Individual Retirement Accounts (IRAs) that offer tax advantages for retirement savings.

- **Traditional IRAs:** Contributions to a traditional IRA may be tax-deductible, meaning taxes are deferred until withdrawal during retirement. This can be advantageous for those expecting to be in a lower tax bracket during retirement.

- **Roth IRAs:** In Roth IRAs, contributions are made with money that has already been taxed, but withdrawals during retirement are tax-free. This can be useful if you expect to be in a higher tax bracket during retirement or if you want to minimize the long-term tax impact.

Planning and Monitoring the Retirement Plan:

Retirement planning is not a one-time event but a continuous process that requires regular monitoring and adjustment.

- **Periodic Review:** It is important to periodically review the retirement plan to ensure it remains aligned with personal goals and circumstances. Changes in tax laws, financial markets, or employment situations may require adjustments to the plan.

- **Diversification of Investments:** Diversifying investments is essential to managing risk and ensuring that the retirement portfolio is robust against market fluctuations. A well-diversified portfolio should include a combination of stocks, bonds, and other financial instruments, spread across different asset classes and sectors.

- **Tax Considerations:** Understanding the tax implications of the retirement plan is crucial to optimizing savings. For example, strategically planning withdrawals to minimize tax impact, or considering converting a traditional IRA to a Roth IRA, can make a significant difference in the long term.

- **Social Security:** Social Security can represent an important part of retirement income, but it should not be the sole source. It is important to understand how Social Security benefits work, when it is optimal to claim them, and how to integrate them into the overall retirement plan.

Managing Risks During Retirement:

During retirement, it is important to manage risks that could compromise the standard of living, such as longevity, inflation, and unexpected healthcare expenses.

- **Longevity:** Living longer than expected

is a real risk, as it could deplete retirement savings. To manage this risk, it may be helpful to consider insurance products like annuities, which offer guaranteed income for life.

- **Inflation:** Inflation can erode purchasing power during retirement. Investments in instruments that offer inflation protection, such as Treasury Inflation-Protected Securities (TIPS), or a percentage of the portfolio invested in stocks, can help counteract this effect.

- **Healthcare Expenses:** Healthcare expenses tend to increase with age and can represent a significant portion of retirement expenses. It is important to plan in advance, considering supplemental health insurance or long-term care plans, to cover these potential needs.

Financial planning in adulthood is a complex process that requires long-term vision and strategic resource management. Setting clear financial goals, creating a solid emergency fund, and carefully planning for retirement are essential steps to ensure financial security and well-being in future years.

A disciplined approach to financial planning, combined with continuous review and adjustment of the plan, can help navigate economic uncertainties and achieve financial peace of mind. Ultimately, effective financial planning is not just about saving and investing, but also about building a solid foundation for a life rich in opportunities and free from financial worries.

5. Debt Management

Debt management is a crucial aspect of personal finance, as debt, if not properly managed, can have serious consequences on financial stability and overall well-being. However, not all debts are the same, and understanding the differences can help make informed decisions and develop effective strategies for managing them. This section explores the different types of debt, strategies for reducing debt, responsible credit use, and financial protection, with a focus on necessary insurance, the importance of a will, and estate planning.

Types of Debt: Good vs. Bad

Good Debt:

"Good debt" is debt that can lead to an increase in net worth or significant improvements in quality of life. This type of debt is considered an investment in the future, as it can generate a positive return in the long term.

- **Mortgage Loans:** One of the most common examples of good debt is a mortgage for purchasing a home. Although it involves a long-term financial commitment, buying property can increase net worth and provide housing stability. Additionally, mortgage interest rates are often lower than other types of debt, and the interest may be tax-deductible in some countries.

- **Student Loans:** Education loans are another example of good debt. Investing in higher education can lead to better job opportunities and increased income over time. However, it is essential to balance the cost of education with the potential return on investment by choosing an educational path that justifies the debt.

- **Business Loans:** Loans for starting or expanding a business can also be considered good debt. If the business is well-planned and has potential for success, the debt can be a means to grow and generate profits. However, it is crucial to carefully evaluate the risks associated with entrepreneurship.

Bad Debt:

"Bad debt" is debt incurred to finance goods or services that do not generate future value or depreciate quickly. This type of debt can quickly become a financial burden, as it does not lead to an increase in net worth or quality of life.

- **Credit Cards:** One of the most common examples of bad debt is credit card debt. Credit cards offer quick access to credit, but high interest rates can cause the debt balance to grow rapidly. If not paid in full each month, credit card debt can become difficult to manage.

- **Consumer Loans:** Loans for consumer goods, such as cars, electronics, or vacations, can be considered bad debt, especially if the item depreciates quickly or does not generate any economic return. For example, buying a new car may seem necessary, but the car depreciates immediately after purchase, making the debt less advantageous.

- **Short-Term Loans and Payday Advances:** These types of loans are often considered bad debt due to their extremely high interest rates and unfavorable repayment terms. They can trap borrowers in a cycle of debt that is difficult to escape.

Strategies for Reducing Debt

Creating a Repayment Plan:

Creating a repayment plan is essential for managing and reducing debt. This plan should include a detailed analysis of existing debt, a priority strategy for repayment, and a long-term commitment to reducing the overall debt balance.

- **Avalanche Method:** This method involves focusing extra payments on the debt with the highest interest rate while maintaining minimum payments on other debts. Once the highest-interest debt is paid off, you move on to the next highest interest rate debt, and so on. This approach minimizes interest paid over time.

- **Snowball Method:** In this method, you focus extra payments on the smallest debt, regardless of interest rate, while maintaining minimum payments on other debts. Once the smallest debt is paid off, you move on to the next smallest debt balance. This method offers a more immediate sense of accomplishment and can be motivating for continuing the debt reduction process.

Debt Consolidation:

Debt consolidation involves combining multiple high-interest debts into a single loan or line of credit with a lower interest rate. This can simplify payments and reduce overall interest paid.

- **Debt Consolidation Loans:** A debt consolidation loan allows you to combine credit card debts, personal loans, and other debts into a single monthly payment. The interest rate on these loans is generally lower than credit card rates, making it easier to manage debt.

- **Balance Transfer Credit Cards:** Some credit cards offer promotional zero or low-interest rates for balance transfers. By transferring balances from high-interest cards to these cards, you can temporarily reduce interest. However, it is essential to pay off the transferred balance before the promotional period ends to avoid high interest rates.

Negotiating with Creditors:

If debt has become difficult to manage, negotiating with creditors can be helpful. Many creditors are willing to work with debtors to find solutions that prevent default.

- **Renegotiating Loan Terms:** In some cases, creditors may be willing to renegotiate loan terms, reduce interest rates, extend the repayment period, or reduce monthly payments. This can make debt more manageable without compromising the credit relationship.

- **Credit Card Repayment Plans:** Some credit card companies offer repayment plans for customers struggling to manage debt. These plans may include a temporary reduction in interest rates or a structured payment plan.

Avoiding New Debt:

To effectively reduce debt, it is essential to avoid taking on new debt. This means living within your means, avoiding impulse purchases, and saving for emergencies instead of relying on credit.

- **Create a Budget:** A well-planned budget can help track expenses and identify areas where savings are possible. This is crucial to avoid incurring new debt.

- **Build an Emergency Fund:** Having an

adequate emergency fund can prevent the need for loans in case of unexpected expenses. This fund should cover at least 3-6 months of essential expenses.

Responsible Credit Use

Understanding How Credit Works:

Responsible credit use requires a deep understanding of how credit works, including how credit scores are calculated, the terms and conditions of credit cards, and the impact of credit on long-term financial health.

- **Credit Score:** A credit score is a measure of a person's creditworthiness, used by creditors to assess the risk of lending. Factors such as timely bill payments, credit utilization, length of credit history, and new credit inquiries affect the score.

- **Interest Rates and Fees:** Credit cards and other credit instruments often carry high interest rates and fees. It is important to understand these costs and try to minimize them by paying the full balance each month or negotiating lower rates with the credit provider.

Responsible Credit Card Use:

Credit cards can be a useful tool if used correctly, but they can also lead to financial problems if not managed responsibly.

- **Paying the Full Balance:** Paying the full balance on your credit card each month is the best way to avoid interest and maintain a healthy credit score. This requires strict spending discipline.

- **Avoiding Maximum Utilization:** Using only a small percentage of your credit limit can help maintain a high credit score and prevent debt problems. It is advisable to keep credit utilization below 30% of the available limit.

- **Tracking Expenses:** Keeping track of

expenses made with a credit card is essential to avoid unpleasant surprises at the end of the month. Many banks offer expense tracking tools that can help with this.

Building Good Credit:

Building good credit takes time and discipline, but it is essential for obtaining favorable loan terms and accessing financial opportunities in the future.

- **Timely Payments:** Payment history is the most important factor in determining your credit score. It is crucial to pay all bills and loans on time every month.

- **Credit Diversification:** Having a variety of types of credit, such as mortgages, car loans, and credit cards, can improve your credit score. However, it is important to manage all debts responsibly.

- **Limiting New Credit Inquiries:** Each

time you apply for new credit, an inquiry is recorded on your credit report, which can temporarily lower your credit score. It is advisable to limit new credit applications to necessary situations.

Financial Protection

Financial protection is a fundamental pillar in managing personal finances, as it allows you to safeguard yourself and your assets against unforeseen events that could compromise financial stability. Financial protection is primarily achieved through adequate insurance and solid estate planning.

Necessary Insurance: Life, Health, Home

Life Insurance:

Life insurance is one of the most important components of financial protection, as it provides financial support to family members in the event of the policyholder's death.

- **Term Life Insurance:** This type of insurance offers coverage for a specific period, usually 10 to 30 years. It is less expensive than whole life insurance and can be used to cover necessary expenses, such as mortgage payments or children's education, if the family breadwinner passes away.

- **Whole Life Insurance:** Unlike term insurance, whole life insurance provides coverage for the entire life of the policyholder. It includes a savings component, known as cash value, that accumulates value over time and can be used by the policyholder as a loan or withdrawal.

- **Universal Life Insurance:** This is a type of permanent life insurance that combines protection and investment. The premium can vary, and a portion of it is invested to accumulate value. It is flexible but more complex and expensive than other policies.

Health Insurance:

Health insurance is essential to protect yourself and your family from unexpected medical expenses, which can be extremely high.

- **Public Health Insurance:** In many countries, public health insurance systems provide coverage for basic medical expenses. However, these systems may have limitations, and many choose to supplement with private insurance.

- **Private Health Insurance:** Private health insurance offers broader coverage and shorter waiting times for treatments. It is particularly useful for those with specific health needs or for those who prefer faster access to medical services.

- **Senior Health Insurance Plans:** As age increases, healthcare costs tend to rise. Specific plans for seniors, such as Medicare in the United States, offer coverage for most medical expenses but may require supplementary insurance to cover costs not included.

Home Insurance:

Home insurance protects one of life's most important investments: your home. It covers damage to the structure and, in some cases, the belongings

inside.

- **Standard Home Insurance:** This insurance typically covers damage caused by fire, theft, vandalism, and certain natural disasters, such as hurricanes and storms. It is essential to read the policy carefully to understand what is covered and what is not.

- **Flood and Earthquake Insurance:** These types of insurance are not usually included in standard policies but are crucial in areas prone to these natural disasters. Flood and earthquake damage can be extensive, and coverage for these events offers critical protection.

- **Renter's Insurance:** Even if you do not own your home, renter's insurance protects your belongings against theft or damage and may also offer liability coverage if someone is injured in your home.

The Importance of a Will

A will is a legal document that outlines how your assets should be distributed after your death. It is a fundamental part of estate planning and ensures that your wishes are respected, reducing the risk of family disputes.

- **Drafting a Will:** Drafting a will involves outlining who will inherit your assets and who will act as the executor of the will, the person responsible for ensuring your wishes are followed. In some cases, it is advisable to include specific instructions regarding the care of minor children.

- **Updating a Will:** A will should be reviewed and updated regularly, especially after major life events such as marriage, divorce, the birth of a child, or significant changes in financial circumstances.

- **Living Will and Power of Attorney:** In addition to a standard will, it is important to consider a living will and a power of attorney for healthcare and financial decisions in the event that you become unable to make decisions on your own.

Estate Planning

Estate planning goes beyond drafting a will and includes all strategies aimed at managing and transferring your assets before and after death. It is essential for reducing tax liabilities, protecting assets, and ensuring that your wishes are respected.

- **Trusts:** Trusts are a useful tool in estate planning, allowing assets to be managed by a trustee for the benefit of the beneficiaries. Trusts can offer tax advantages, protect assets from creditors, and ensure that assets are distributed according to your wishes.

- **Tax Planning:** Estate planning includes strategies for minimizing estate and inheritance taxes. Consulting with a financial advisor or tax professional is essential to ensure that you are using the most effective strategies.

- **Charitable Donations:** If philanthropy is important to you, estate planning can include provisions for donating a portion of your estate to charity. This can also provide tax benefits.

- **Asset Protection:** Estate planning can also involve strategies for protecting your assets from potential creditors or legal actions.

This may include setting up trusts or other legal entities to hold assets.

Effective debt management and financial protection are essential components of a secure and prosperous financial future. By understanding the differences between good and bad debt, implementing strategies for debt reduction, using credit responsibly, and ensuring proper insurance coverage and estate planning, individuals can protect themselves and their loved ones from financial hardship and build a legacy of stability and prosperity.

6.Investments and Capital Growth

Investing is a fundamental pillar for capital growth and long-term financial planning. Understanding financial markets, analyzing various types of investments, and adapting to emerging trends are essential for building and maintaining a solid financial base. In this section, we will explore how financial markets operate, strategies for analyzing and monitoring portfolios, and opportunities offered by modern trends such as ethical investments, technological innovations, and emerging markets.

Financial Markets and Investments

How Financial Markets Work

Financial markets are platforms where goods

and financial instruments, such as stocks, bonds, currencies, and derivatives, are traded. These markets facilitate capital mobilization, price discovery, and risk management.

- **Structure of Financial Markets:**

Financial markets are primarily divided into two categories: primary and secondary markets.

- **Primary Markets:** In these markets, new issues of securities, such as stocks and bonds, are sold for the first time to investors. This process is known as an initial public offering (IPO) for stocks and a bond offering for debt securities. Companies and governments use primary markets to raise funds for expansions, projects, or other capital needs.

- **Secondary Markets:** After the initial sale, securities are traded between investors in the secondary market. Stock exchanges like the New York Stock Exchange (NYSE) and NASDAQ are examples of secondary markets where stocks and other financial instruments are bought and sold daily. The secondary market provides liquidity to investors and facilitates the ongoing valuation of financial instruments.

- **Types of Markets:**

  - **Stock Markets:** Places where shares of publicly traded companies are bought and sold. The valuation of stocks is influenced by various factors, including company performance, economic conditions, and future expectations.

  - **Bond Markets:** Here, bonds, which are debt securities issued by governments or companies, are traded. Investors purchase bonds to receive fixed income in the form of interest. Bonds can vary in risk and return depending on the issuer's credit rating.

  - **Derivative Markets:** Derivatives are financial instruments whose value derives from another asset, such as stocks, bonds, currencies, or commodities. Examples include futures and options. Derivative markets are used for speculation and risk hedging.

  - **Currency Markets:** Known as Forex

(Foreign Exchange), these markets facilitate the exchange of currencies. Exchange rates between currencies are influenced by economic, political, and market factors.

- **Price Mechanisms:**

Prices in financial markets are determined by the interaction of supply and demand. When the demand for a security exceeds supply, the price tends to rise, and vice versa. Security prices reflect investors' expectations regarding the future economic and financial performance of a company or a bond issuer.

Fundamental and Technical Analysis

Fundamental and technical analyses are two primary approaches to evaluating and deciding on investments.

- **Fundamental Analysis:**

Fundamental analysis focuses on evaluating

the intrinsic value of an investment by examining economic, financial, and business conditions. Fundamental analysts study financial statements, growth prospects, and economic factors to determine whether a security is undervalued or overvalued.

- **Financial Statements:** Analysts examine a company's financial statements to assess its financial health, analyzing indicators such as earnings per share (EPS), price-to-earnings ratio (P/E), profit margin, and capital structure.

- **Growth Prospects:** Consideration is given to the company's future prospects, including expansion plans, innovation, and competitiveness in the industry.

- **Macro-Economic Factors:** Analysts also evaluate the impact of general economic conditions, such as interest rates, inflation, and economic growth, on the value of investments.

- **Technical Analysis:**

Technical analysis relies on examining historical market data, such as prices and trading volumes, to forecast future price movements. Technical analysts use charts and technical indicators to identify market trends and patterns.

- **Charts and Indicators:** Analysts use charts to visualize price movements over time and technical indicators like moving averages, the relative strength index (RSI), and Bollinger Bands to make trading decisions.

- **Price Patterns:** Technical analysis is based on price patterns, such as head and shoulders, triangles, and channels, which help identify potential trend reversals and trading opportunities.

- **Trading Volume:** Trading volume can confirm trends and price reversals. An increase in volume during a price movement may indicate greater investor conviction.

Portfolio Monitoring and Review

Regular monitoring and review of a portfolio are essential to ensure that investments continue to meet financial goals and to make adjustments in response to market changes.

- **Rebalancing:** Rebalancing involves adjusting the portfolio composition to maintain the desired asset allocation. Over time, some asset classes may grow faster than others, altering the original proportion. Rebalancing helps keep the portfolio's risk and return in line with the goals.

- **Performance Evaluation:** Monitoring investment performance against benchmarks and set goals allows for the assessment of whether investments are performing as expected. If an investment is not meeting expectations, it may be necessary to consider adjustments.

- **Updating Goals:** Financial goals may change over time due to personal or economic circumstances. It is important to regularly update goals and adjust investment strategies accordingly.

Investing Based on Trends

Ethical and Sustainable Investments

In recent years, there has been growing interest in ethical and sustainable investments, which focus on companies and projects that promote responsible environmental, social, and governance practices.

- **Socially Responsible Investments (SRI):** SRI focuses on companies that meet ethical criteria, such as human rights, labor practices, and environmental sustainability. SRI investors avoid sectors considered harmful, such as tobacco, weapons, and fossil fuels.

- **Environmental, Social, and Governance (ESG) Investments:** ESG investments evaluate companies based on their environmental, social, and governance impacts. Companies with high ESG ratings tend to show better management of risks and opportunities related to these aspects and may offer better long-term financial performance.

- **Sustainable Funds:** Many investment funds and ETFs now offer sustainable options that select companies based on ESG criteria. These funds allow investors to support responsible business practices without compromising financial returns.

Technological Innovations and Their Impact

Technological innovations are revolutionizing financial markets and creating new investment opportunities. Emerging technologies such as artificial intelligence (AI), blockchain, and fintech are changing the investment landscape.

- **Artificial Intelligence (AI):** AI is used to analyze vast amounts of financial data and make more accurate market predictions. Algorithmic trading platforms use AI to make investment decisions based on predictive models and advanced algorithms.

- **Blockchain and Cryptocurrencies:** Blockchain technology supports cryptocurrencies like Bitcoin and Ethereum. Cryptocurrencies offer new investment possibilities and have the potential to transform the financial sector through decentralization and enhanced transaction security.

- **Fintech:** Fintech startups are changing how investors access financial services, offering online trading platforms, robo-advisors, and innovative payment solutions. These technologies improve investment access and efficiency.

Emerging Markets and Future Opportunities

Emerging markets offer significant growth opportunities but come with higher risks compared to developed markets.

- **Economic Growth:** Emerging markets, such as those in Asia, Latin America, and Africa, often exhibit faster growth rates than developed markets. These countries are frequently experiencing rapid urbanization and industrialization, creating investment opportunities in sectors like infrastructure, consumer goods, and technology.

- **Diversification:** Investing in emerging markets can help diversify a portfolio, reducing overall risk and increasing potential returns. However, it is important to consider associated risks, such as political and economic volatility.

- **Sector Opportunities:** Emerging sectors like green technology, renewable energy, and healthcare innovation offer substantial growth opportunities. Investors should seek out high-growth potential sectors and develop strategies to capitalize on these trends.

Investments and capital growth are fundamental to building strong financial security. Understanding how financial markets operate, using fundamental and technical analyses to make informed decisions, and staying updated on emerging trends are crucial steps for investment success. Adapting to technological innovations, opportunities in emerging markets, and sustainable investments can offer significant advantages and contribute to a more secure and prosperous financial future.

7. Behavior and Economic Psychology

Economic psychology explores how emotions and mental processes influence financial decisions and consumption behaviors. This discipline combines elements of psychology and economics to understand how people make decisions regarding money and resources and how these behaviors can be affected by cognitive biases, self-control, and impulses.

Consumer Psychology

Consumer Behavior

Consumer behavior studies how and why people choose to purchase goods and services. This field examines various aspects, including the factors influencing purchase decisions and consumption habits.

- **Purchase Decision Process:** The consumer decision-making process often includes several stages:

  - **Need Recognition:** The process begins when a consumer recognizes a need or desire. This may stem from a practical necessity or a more emotional or social desire.

  - **Information Search:** After recognizing a need, the consumer searches for information about available products or services. This search can include consulting online sources, product reviews, and advice from friends and family.

  - **Evaluation of Alternatives:** Consumers compare the various options available, weighing the pros and cons of each. This may involve evaluating prices, features, and product performance.

  - **Purchase Decision:** After evaluating the alternatives, the consumer makes a purchase decision based on the criteria deemed most important. This can include considerations such as price, quality, brand, and availability.

  - **Post-Purchase Behavior:** After the purchase, the consumer assesses whether their expectations have been met. Post-purchase satisfaction or dissatisfaction can influence future decisions and word-of-mouth.

- **Factors Influencing Purchase Behavior:**

  - **Personal Factors:** Age, income, occupation, and lifestyle influence purchasing decisions. For example, young people may be more attracted to innovative tech products, while families with children might seek practical and durable goods.

  - **Psychological Factors:** Personal motivations, perceptions, and attitudes play a crucial role. Maslow's hierarchy of needs theory, for example, suggests that more basic needs must be met before people seek goods and services that fulfill higher needs like self-actualization.

  - **Social Factors:** Social influences, such as the behavior of friends and family, group trends, and advertising campaigns, can significantly impact purchasing decisions. Social norms and cultural expectations often guide consumer choices.

 - **Environmental Factors:** The shopping environment, including store layouts, product placement, and overall customer experience, can influence purchasing behavior. Marketing strategies like special offers and attractive displays can encourage purchases.

Cognitive Biases and Financial Decisions

Cognitive biases are systematic errors in thinking that affect decision-making. These biases can lead to suboptimal financial decisions and irrational consumption behaviors.

 - **Anchoring Bias:** This bias occurs when people rely on an initial piece of information (the anchor) to make subsequent decisions. For example, if a consumer sees a high price for a product and then finds a slightly lower price, they may perceive it as a bargain, even if the final price is still high.

- **Confirmation Bias:** People tend to seek out and give more weight to information that confirms their preexisting beliefs while ignoring information that contradicts them. This can lead to poor financial decisions if an investor only looks for data supporting a preexisting belief about a stock or company.

- **Endowment Effect:** Individuals attribute a higher value to objects they own compared to those they do not. This bias can influence selling decisions, leading to higher selling prices than the perceived market value.

- **Loss Aversion:** People tend to fear losses more than they value equivalent gains. This bias can lead to conservative behaviors and suboptimal financial decisions, such as holding onto losing investments to avoid realizing a loss.

- **Overconfidence Bias:** Individuals may overestimate their ability to predict and control future events. This bias can lead to risky investment decisions and overly optimistic behavior.

- **Availability Bias:** Decisions can be influenced by how easily information comes to mind. If a recent event has been widely reported, people might overestimate the likelihood of it happening again, affecting their investment or consumption decisions.

Self-Discipline and Impulsivity

Self-discipline and impulsivity are two fundamental dimensions of financial behavior that affect one's ability to manage money and make informed financial choices.

- **Self-Discipline:**

- **Budget Management:** Self-discipline is crucial for adhering to a budget plan and sticking to spending limits. Disciplined individuals tend to plan expenses, save regularly, and avoid impulsive purchases.

- **Long-Term Financial Goals:** The ability to delay gratification and focus on long-term financial goals is a key characteristic of self-discipline. This may include saving for retirement, paying off debt, or building an emergency fund.

- **Preventing Excessive Spending:** Individuals with strong self-discipline can resist the temptation of unnecessary spending and maintain a balance between immediate expenses and future needs.

- **Impulsivity:**

  - **Impulse Purchases:** Impulsivity can lead to unplanned and unnecessary spending. Impulsive people may be more susceptible to promotions and advertisements that offer immediate gratification.

  - **Lack of Planning:** Impulsive

individuals may struggle with planning and sticking to a budget, often spending more than they earn and accumulating debt.

 - **Strategies to Manage Impulsivity:** Creating a spending plan, using budgeting techniques, and delaying purchase decisions can help reduce impulsivity and improve financial management.

Financial Education for New Generations

Financial education is crucial for preparing new generations to manage money effectively and make informed financial decisions. Teaching children and young adults about the value of money and financial skills can have a lasting impact on their adult lives.

10.1 Teaching Children the Value of Money

Teaching children the value of money from a young age is essential for developing healthy financial habits.

- **Basic Money Concepts:**

  - **Origin of Money:** Explaining to children where money comes from and how it is earned through work can help them understand its value.

  - **Money Management:** Teaching children how to manage money through saving, spending, and investing. Children can start to understand the difference between needs and wants and learn to make informed choices.

- **Chores and Rewards:**

  - **Compensation System:** Using a reward system for chores can help children understand that money is earned through work. This system can teach them the value of money and the concept of saving.

- **Saving Management:** Encouraging children to set aside a portion of their money for future purchases or specific goals can promote the habit of saving and financial planning.

- **Using Games and Activities:**

  - **Educational Games:** Board games and market simulations can teach children fundamental concepts of economics and finance in an interactive and engaging way.

  - **Practical Activities:** Practical activities such as setting up a "home bank" or managing a small budget for a project can help children apply financial skills.

10.2 Tools and Resources for Educators and Parents

Educators and parents have a variety of tools and resources available to teach financial education to young people.

- **Financial Education Programs and Courses:**

  - **School Programs:** Some schools and organizations offer financial education programs covering topics such as budgeting, debt management, and investing. These programs can be integrated into the school curriculum to provide comprehensive training.

  - **Online Courses and Educational Resources:** There are numerous online courses and educational resources available to help educators and parents teach financial skills. These courses can provide teaching materials, practical activities, and strategies to engage young people.

- **Interactive Tools:**

  - **Budgeting Apps for Kids:** Several apps are designed to help children manage their money interactively. These apps may include features such as expense tracking, goal saving, and educational games.

  - **Educational Games and Simulations:** Games and simulations can offer a hands-on experience in money and finance management, making learning more engaging and enjoyable.

- **Educational Materials:**

  - **Books and Guides:** There are books and guides designed to teach financial education to young people. These materials can provide clear and simple explanations of complex financial concepts.

  - **Activities and Workshops:** Creating activities and workshops can help young people understand financial concepts through practical and interactive experiences.

10.3 The Importance of Financial Literacy in Schools

Incorporating financial education into the school curriculum is essential for preparing students to manage their finances in the future.

- **Benefits of Financial Education:**

  - **Skill Development:** Financial education helps students develop essential skills such as budgeting, debt management, and investing. These skills are crucial for a financially healthy life.

  - **Preventing Financial Problems:** Providing students with the necessary skills and knowledge can help prevent future financial issues, such as debt accumulation and lack of savings.

  - **Preparation for the Future:** Students who receive adequate financial education are better prepared to face the financial challenges of adulthood, such as managing daily expenses, planning for retirement, and managing investments.

- **Curriculum Implementation:**

  - **Integration into Existing Programs:** Financial education can be integrated into existing school programs, such as social sciences and economics. This approach allows for financial training without requiring a complete curriculum overhaul.

- **Initiatives and Projects:** Schools can implement special initiatives and projects, such as financial clubs and budgeting competitions, to engage students and make learning more dynamic and interactive.

Economic psychology and financial education are two crucial areas for understanding and improving personal financial management. Awareness of cognitive biases and the management of self-discipline are essential for making more rational and informed financial decisions. Additionally, financial education for new generations plays a fundamental role in preparing young people to manage money effectively and responsibly. Investing in financial education from a young age and using appropriate tools and resources can help build a strong foundation for future financial success.

8. Financial Education Glossary

1. Asset

An asset is anything of value or a resource owned by an individual or entity that is expected to provide future economic benefits. Examples include real estate, stocks, and personal property.

2. Budget

A budget is a financial plan that outlines expected income and expenditures over a specific period, such as a month or year. It helps individuals or organizations manage their finances and achieve financial goals.

3. Debt

Debt is an amount of money borrowed by an individual or organization that must be repaid, usually with interest. Common types of debt include loans, mortgages, and credit card balances.

4. Emergency Fund

An emergency fund is a savings account set aside for unexpected expenses or financial emergencies, such as medical bills or car repairs. It provides a financial safety net.

5. Income

Income refers to the money received by an individual or entity from various sources, such as wages, salaries, investments, or business profits. It is used to cover living expenses and achieve financial goals.

6. Interest

Interest is the cost of borrowing money or the return on invested capital. It is typically expressed as a percentage of the principal amount and can be either simple or compound.

7. Investment

An investment is an asset or item acquired with the goal of generating income or appreciating in value over time. Investments can include stocks, bonds, real estate, and mutual funds.

8. Liability

A liability is a financial obligation or debt that an individual or organization owes to others. Examples include loans, mortgages, and unpaid bills.

9. Net Worth

Net worth is the difference between an individual's or entity's total assets and total liabilities. It provides a snapshot of financial health and wealth.

10. Savings

Savings refers to money set aside from income for future use. It can be held in various forms, such as savings accounts, certificates of deposit, or retirement accounts.

11. Credit Score

A credit score is a numerical representation of an individual's creditworthiness, based on their credit history and financial behavior. It affects the ability to obtain loans and the terms of credit.

12. Financial Planning

Financial planning is the process of setting financial goals, creating strategies to achieve them, and managing resources to ensure financial stability and success.

13. Retirement Fund

A retirement fund is a savings or investment account set up to provide income during retirement. Common retirement funds include 401(k) plans, IRAs, and pensions.

14. Risk Management

Risk management involves identifying, assessing, and prioritizing financial risks and taking steps to mitigate or manage them. It includes strategies like insurance and diversification.

15. Taxation

Taxation is the process by which governments collect money from individuals and businesses to fund public services and infrastructure. It includes various forms of taxes, such as income tax, sales tax, and property tax.

16. Diversification

Diversification is a risk management strategy that involves spreading investments across different assets or asset classes to reduce the impact of any single investment's poor performance.

17. Compound Interest

Compound interest is interest calculated on the initial principal and also on the accumulated interest from previous periods. It allows investments to grow at an accelerated rate over time.

18. Liquidity

Liquidity refers to the ease with which an asset can be converted into cash without significantly affecting its value. Cash is the most liquid asset, while real estate is less liquid.

19. Financial Literacy

Financial literacy is the knowledge and understanding of financial concepts and principles, including budgeting, investing, and managing debt. It is essential for making informed financial decisions.

20. Portfolio

A portfolio is a collection of investments owned by an individual or organization. It may include a variety of asset types, such as stocks, bonds, and real estate, to achieve specific financial goals.

21. Inflation

Inflation is the rate at which the general level of prices for goods and services rises, eroding purchasing power. It can impact savings, investments, and overall financial planning.

22. Goal Setting

Goal setting involves defining specific, measurable, achievable, relevant, and time-bound (SMART) financial objectives. It helps individuals and organizations stay focused and motivated to achieve their financial goals.

23. Mortgage

A mortgage is a loan used to purchase real estate, where the property serves as collateral for the loan. It typically involves regular payments of principal and interest over a specified term.

24. Fixed Expenses

Fixed expenses are regular, predictable costs that do not change from month to month, such as rent or mortgage payments, insurance premiums, and subscription services.

25. Variable Expenses

Variable expenses are costs that can fluctuate in amount and frequency, such as groceries, entertainment, and dining out. They can be adjusted based on changes in income and financial goals.

26. Wealth Management

Wealth management is a comprehensive financial service that involves managing an individual's or family's investments, estate planning, tax strategies, and other financial needs to grow and preserve wealth.

27. Estate Planning

Estate planning is the process of arranging for

the distribution of an individual's assets after their death. It involves creating wills, trusts, and other legal documents to ensure that assets are distributed according to one's wishes.

28. Mutual Fund

A mutual fund is an investment vehicle that pools money from multiple investors to invest in a diversified portfolio of stocks, bonds, or other assets. It is managed by professional fund managers.

29. Roth IRA

A Roth IRA is a retirement savings account that allows individuals to contribute after-tax income, with the benefit of tax-free withdrawals in retirement. Contributions are not tax-deductible, but earnings grow tax-free.

30. 401(k) Plan

A 401(k) plan is a employer-sponsored retirement savings plan that allows employees to contribute a portion of their salary on a pre-tax or after-tax basis. Employers may also provide matching contributions.

This glossary provides key terms and concepts to enhance understanding of financial education and management.

Index

1. Introduction pg.4

2. Basic Principles of Personal Finance pg.20

3. Types of Savings and Investments pg.34

4. Financial Planning in Adulthood pg.49

5. Debt Management pg.63

6. Investments and Capital Growth pg.81

7. Behavior and Economic Psychology pg.93

8. Financial Education Glossary pg.107

www.ingramcontent.com/pod-product-compliance
Lightning Source LLC
Chambersburg PA
CBHW071058240526
45471CB00016B/2152